One Moment on Earth

OrangeBooks Publication

1st Floor, Rajhans Arcade, Mall Road, Kohka, Bhilai, Chhattisgarh 490020

Website: **www.orangebooks.in**

First Edition, 2024

ONE MOMENT ON EARTH

PRAMOD M TIPPASHETTI

OrangeBooks Publication

www.orangebooks.in

Introduction

An ordinary person's perspective of the earth for a moment. Ever changing world, more older, ever newer world. To pause for a moment & look into things & wonder, to live better.

If we assume to be the world is paused for a moment. We see the world is full of living beings & nonliving things. Being alive, being human, living in modern human society, perspective of the world may appear differently.

The world with life, plants, trees, animals, birds, etc. The life keep happening, self-sustainable nature keep being alive, fresh & going through life cycles. Being ordinary person, thinking of the world with nature & life, makes us wonder & makes us to search for the answers to happenings. To know the creation & existence, we search for the creator. We are part of the creator's creation, after understanding this basic thing only then we can find the peace & happiness. The surrenderedness & devotion can show us creator & his wonderful creation, purpose of everything. Creator in deeper level & silence, playfulness in his own creation. We can only explore his vast creation, experience new things, we can live & enjoy for some time.

Contents

Creator & Creativity

Creator & Creation

"Aadi Ananta Shiva" Lord Shiva is worshipped as creator, the start, endless & ender of the creation. In India & many other cultures Lord Shiva is admired to be the creator. The Creation is manly by five elements, Sky, Fire, Water, Air, Earth, the creation components are also worshipped as panchabhutas. The creation or the existence is the creator's creativity.

Here the creation is the Sun, Earth, Moon, Solar System in the Universe. Every creation will be having its own working mechanism depending on creator's creativity. The creator or sub ordinate of the creator might have lived from ancient times as some civilization or being guiding lights to the civilization. Every civilization will be having hierarchy or levels of the society. The top level of hierarchy will be aware of the creator's presence, will have been guided by the creator or sub-ordinates. The working mechansion of the creation, the purpose of the creation, the maintanance of the creation, understanding the geological conditions & dependence, the way of living might have been passed from generations as cultures or tradition. The creator has guided the top level of societies.

Even in todays generation the way of living is passed from generation is guidance given by creator or sub ordinates in one or other form. Across the world different religions, different cultures, different traditions but worshipping the creator & creation in many different ways according to their ancestors given knowledge. There ancestors or top level of Societies will have been guided or blessed by the creator.

The creator might have lived in many forms. The hierarchy of a society will have level, top level, middle level, low level. The creators will be available for all levels of the society living in his creation. Will be guiding or blessing according to their deeds & needs.

The creation will be maintained by the subordinates of the creator or by the creator himself. In the path of enlightment there is a theory of Brahma, Vishnu, Mahesh as the Creator, Maintainer, Destroyer of the creation or universe.

Creator is the one, by living in his own creation, giving life to many life beings, setting standards of living, changing according to his vision. Creation or the universe is huge, there are so many levels or dimensions have been created by the creator. The people who will be owning particular spaces in the creation at different levels will be having access to their lower dimension. The creator will be having access to all the levels with different dimension being only one at highest dimension.

The people who will be owning some spaces in the vast creation, will be having their own set of standards of living or civilization. They might have lived from ancient times & continue to living many more years ahead.

Their intelligence will be more compared to the ordinary people living on planet Earth. Considering the creation in the universe, time will not be the same as on earth. The planets might be having different rotation speeds, different temperatures according to their stars. The age of living might be more than compared to living on Earth. Hence the Intelligent being will be living longer lifes than normal humans on Earth.

In the creation or universe, the subordinates of creator who will be maintaining the larger spaces of universe will be able to multitasking, will be having higher Intelligence in creativity.

Depending on the power of creation level there are some assumption of levels.

Creator Civilization

The highest level of the creator, involving the process of creation of universes, stars, planets, etc. The creator having the control of entire creation, having the access to all the life beings of creation. The creator living in his own creation giving the knowledge to ordinary life beings, giving chance to explore his creation. The creation & Destruction of the creation is carried by the creator himself ; is the main thing of the Creator civilization.

Multidimensional Civilization

Creator living in his own creation, creating something new & again living in his own creation is travelling form larger size to smaller size in his own creation, this explains the multidimensional civilization. In every different dimension the civilizations will be following their standards, knowledge given by creator in some form. The creator will be visiting different dimension in some or other from according to his vision whenever it is required. The creator will be giving power of creation according to dimension to maintain the societies in good conditions, utilizing it for the fulfill of the little needs & betterment of society. The knowledge & power receivers are assumed to be super intelligent beings. Intelligent being who will be guiding the civilization or societies. The creator or sub ordinates as supreme beings will descend from sky to planet to give knowledge & guide societies whenever it is required.

Big Bang

The Big Bang event is a physical theory that describes how the universe expanded from an initial state of high density & temperature. It was first proposed in 1927 by Roman catholic priest & phycisist Georges Lemostre. Various cosmological models of the Big Bang explain the evolution of observable universe. From the earliest known periods through its subsequent large scale from. These models offer a comprehensive explanation for a broad range of observed pheromena, including the abundance of light elements, the cosmic microwave background (CMB) radiation & large scale structure. The overall uniformity of the universe, known as the flatten problem is explained through cosmic inflation a sudden & very rapid expansion of space during the earliest moments. However physics currently lacks a widely accepted theory of quantum gravity that can successfully model the earliest condition of the Big Bang.

Crucially, these models are compatible with the hubble - Lemairtre law the observation that farther away a galaxy is, the farter it is moving away from Earth Extrapolating this cosmic expansion backwards in time using the known laws of physics, the models describe or increasingly concentrated cosmos preceded by a singularity in which space & time lose meaning (typically named "the Big Bang singularity") In 1964 the CMB was discovered. Which convinced many cosmologists that the competing steady - state model of cosmic evolution was falsified, since the Big Bang models predict a uniform background radiation caused by high temperature & densities in the distant past. A wide range of empuseal evidence strongly favors the Big Bang event, which is now essentially universally accepted. Detailed measurements of the expansion rate of the universe place the Big Bang singularity at on estimated 13.787 billion year ago, which is considered the age of the universe.

There remain aspects of the observed universe that one not yet adequately explained by the Big Bang models. After its initial expansion, the universe cooled sufficiently to allow the formation of subatomic particle & later atoms. The unequal abundances of matter & antimatter that allowed this to occur is an unexplained effect known as baryon asymmetry. These primordial element - mostly hydrogen, with some helium & lithium later coalesced through gravity, forming early stars & galaxies. Astronomer observe the gravitational effects of on unknown dank another surrounding galaxies. Astronomer observe the gravitational effects of an unknown dark matter surrounding galaxies. Most of the gravitational potential in the universe seems to be in this from, & the Big Bang models & various observations indicate that this execs gravitational potential is not created by baryonic matter, such or normal atoms. Measurements of the redshifts of supernova indicate that expansion of the universe in accelerating, an observation attributed to an unexplained phenomenon known as dark energy.

Creativity

Creativity is a characters of someone or some process that forms something new & valuable. The created them may intangible (such as an idea, a scientific theory, a musical composition, or a joke) or a physical object (such as invention, printed literary work or a painting.)

Scholarly interest in creativity is found in a number of disciplines, primarily psychology, business studies & cognitive science However it is also present in education, the humanities (including philosophy & arts) theology social sciences (such as sociology, linguistics, economics) as well as in engineering, technology & mathematics. These disciplines cover the relation between creativity & general intelligence. Personality type, mental & Neural processes, mental health & artificial intelligence, the potential for fostering creativity through education, training, leadership & organization practices, the factor that determine how creativity is evaluated & perceived; the fostering of creativity for national economic benefit; & the application of creative resources to improve the effectiveness of teaching & learning. Creativity enables us to solve problems in new or innovation ways. According to harverd business school, it benefits business by encouraging innovation, boosting productivity, enabling adaptability & fostering growth.

Earth

Earth is the third planet from the Sun & the Only Planet or astronomical object known to harbor life. This is enabled by Earth being a water world. The only planet in the Solar system sustaining liquid surface water. Almost all of Earth's water is contained in its global ocean, covering 70.8 % of Earth's Crust. The remaining 29.2% Earth's crust is Land. Land is in the from of continental land masses, earth land hemisphere. Most of Earth's land is somewhat humid & covered by vegetation. Earth's polar regions are covered by ice deserts, retain more water than Earth's ground water, lakes, rivers & atmosphere water combined. Earth's crust consists of slowly moving tectonic plates, which interact to produce mountain ranges, volcanoes & earthquakes. Earth has a liquid outer core that generates magnetosphere capable of deflecting most of the disruptive solar winds & cosmic radiation.

Earth has a dynamic atmosphere, which sustains Earth's surface condition & protects it from most meteoroids & UV- light at entry. It has a composition of primarily nitrogen & oxygen. Water vapor is widely present in the atmosphere. Water vapor is also present in the from of cloud that covers most of the planet. The water vapor acts as a green house gas & together with other green house gases in the atmosphere, particularly Carbon dioxide (CO_2), creates the condition for both liquid surface water & water vapor to persist via the capturing of energy from the sunlight. This process maintains the current average surface temperature of 14.76^0C, at which water is liquid under atmosphere pressure. Differences in the amount of captured energy between geographic regions (as with the equatorial region receiving more sunlight than the polar regions) drives the atmosphere & ocean currents, producing a global climate system, with different climate regions and a range of weather phenomena such as precipetition allowing components such as Nitrogen to cycle.

Earth is rounded in to an ellipsoid with a circumference of about 40,000 km. it is the densest planet in the solar system. Earth is about eight light minutes away from the Sun. Earth orbit around the Sun taking 365 days to complete one revolution. Earth rotated around its own axis in 24 hours. Earth's axis of rotation is tilted with respect to the perpendicular to its orbital plane around the Sun, about 23.5^0 causing the seasons on Earth. Earth is orbited by one permanent natural satellite, the Moon, which orbits earth at 3,84,400 km & is roughly a quarter as wide Earth. The moon's gravity helps stabilize Earth's axis, & also causes tides which gradually slows earth's rotation. As a result of tidal locking, the same side of the Moon always faces Earth.

Earth, like most other bodies on the Solar system, formed 4.5 billion years ago from gas in the early solar system. During the first billion years of Earth's formation, the ocean formed & then life developed within it, life spread globally & has been altering Earths's atmosphere & surface, leading to the great oxidation event two billion years ago. Humans emerged 3,00,000 years ago on land & have spread across the globe with the exception of Antarctica. Human depend on Earth's biosphere & natural resources for their survival, but have increasingly impacted the planet's environment. Humanity's current impact on Earth's climate &biosphere is unsustainable, threatening the livelihood of human & many other form of life & causing widespread extinctions.

Orbit & Rotation

Rotation

Earth's rotation period relative to the Sun - its mean solar day - is 86,400,seconds of mean solar time. Because Earth's solar day is now slightly longer than it was during the 19th century due to tidal deceleration, each day varies between 0 & 2 ms longer than the mean solar day.

Earth's rotation period relative to the fixed stars, called its stellar day the international Earth Rotation & reference Systems Services (IERS) 86,164,0989 second of mean solar time or 23^h 56^m 4.0989^s. Earth rotation period relative to the processing or moving mean march equinox (when the Sun is at 90^0 On the equator) is 86,164.0905 seconds of mean solar time (UTI) 23^h 56^m 4.0905^s. This the sidereal day is shorter than the stellar a by about 8.4 ms.

Apart from meteors within the atmosphere &low orbiting satellites, the main apparent motion of celestial bodies in Earth's sky is to the west at a rate of $15^0/n =$ $15^1/min$ for bodies near the celestial equator, this is equivalent to an opponent diameter of the Sun on the

Moon every two minutes. From Earths Surface the apparent sizes of the Sun & the Moon are approximately the same.

Orbit

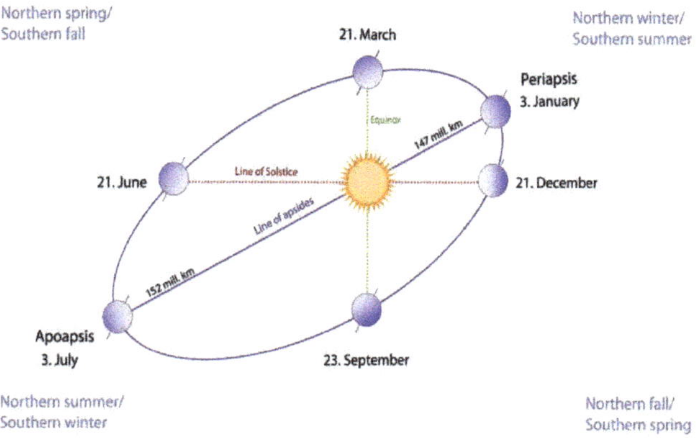

Earth orbits the Sun, being third planet from the Sun & part of inner solar system. Earth's average orbital distance is about 150 million km. which is the basis of the astronomical unit & is equal to roughly 8.3 light minutes or 380 times Earth's distance to the Moon.

Earth orbits the Sun every 365.2564 mean solar days. With apparent movement of the Sun in Earth's sky at a rate of about 1^0/day eastward, which is one apparent Sun or Moon diameter every 12 hours. Due to this motion, on Earth to complete a full rotation about its axis so that the Sun returns to the meridian. The orbital speed of Earth averages about 29.78 km/s (1,07,200 km/h).

The Moon & Earth orbit a common bary center every 27.32 days relative to the background stars. When combined with the Earth - Moon system's common Orbit the around the Sun, the period of synodic moon. from new moon to new moon, is 29.53 days Earth's axis is tilted some 23.44 degrees from the perpendralor to the Earth - Sun plane & the Earth - Moon plane is tilted up to 15.1 degrees against the Earth - Sun plane without this tilt, there would be an eclipse every two weeks, alternating between lunar eclipses & solar eclipses.

The Hill sphere or the sphere of gravitational influence of Earth is about 1.5 million km in radius. This is the maximum distance at which Earth's gravitational influence is stronger than the more distant Sun & Planets. Objects must orbit Earth within this radius, on they can become unbound by gravitational perturbation of the Sun.

Axial tilt & Seasons

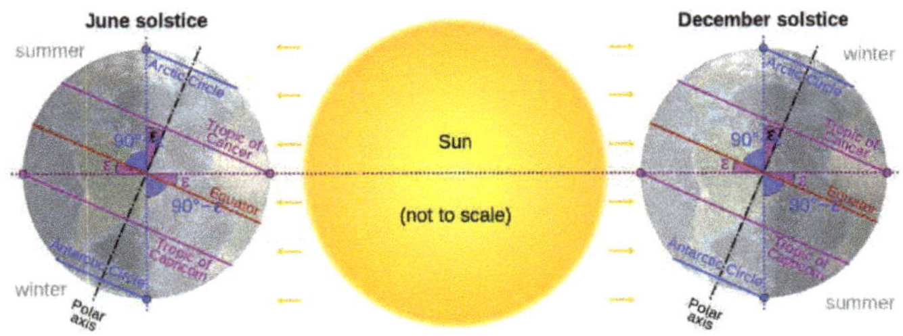

The axial tilt of the Earth is approximately 23.439281^0 with the axis of its orbit plane, always pointing towards the celestial poles. Due to Earth's axial tilt, the amount of sunlight reaching any given point surface vases over the course of the year. This causes the seasonal changes in climate, with summer in the northern hemisphere occuring when the tropic of cancer is facing the Sun, & in the southern hemisphere when the tropic of Capricorn faces the Sun. In each instance, winter occurs simultaneously in the opposite hemisphere.

During the Summer, the day lasts longer & the Sun climbs higher in the sky. In winter, the climate becomes colder & day shorter. Above the Arctic circle & below the Antarctic circle there is no daylight at all for part of the year, causing a polar night & this night extends for several months at the poles themselves. There same latitudes also experience a midnight Sun, where Sun remains visible all day.

By astronomical convention, the four seasons can be determined by the solstices the points in the orbit of maximum axial tilt toward or away from the Sun & the equinoxes, when Earths rotational axis is alligned with its orbital axis. In the northern thermosphere winter solstice currently occurs around 21 December, Summer solstice is near 21 June, spring equinox is around 20 march & autumnal equinox is about 22 or 23 September. In the Southern Hemisphere, the situation is reversed ,& with the summer & winter solstices exchanged & the spring & autumnal equinox dates swapped.

In modern times, Earth's perihellion occurs around 3 January & its aphelion around 4 July. These dates changes over time due to precession & other orbital factors, which follow cyclical patterns known as milankovitch cycles. The changing Earth - Sun distance causes an increase of about 6.8 % in solar energy reaching Earth at perihelion relative to aphelion. Because the southern hemisphere is tilted toward the Sun at about the some time that Earth reaches the closest approach to the Sun, the southern hemisphere receives slightly more energy from the Sun than does the northern over the course of a year. This effect is much less significant than the total energy change due to the casual tilt & most of the excess energy is absorbed by the highest proportion of water in the southern hemisphere.

Earth – Moon System

Moon

The Moon is relatively large, terrestrial planet like natural satellite, with a diameter about one - quarter of Earth's. It is the largest moon in the solar system relative to the size of its planet situated at 3,84,000 km from Earth. Charon is larger relative to the dwarf planet Pluto. The natural satellites of other Planets are also referenced to as "Moons", after Earth's. The most widely accepted theory of the Moon's origin, the giant impact hypothesis, states that it formed from the collisions of a Mars - size protoplanet called Theia with the early Earth. This hypothesis explains the Moon's relative look of iron & volatile elements & the fact that its composition is nearly identical to that of Earth's crust.

The gravitational attraction between Earth & the Moon causes tides on Earth. The some effect on the Moon has led to its Tidal locking. Its rotation period is the same as the time it takes to orbit Earth. As a result, it always presents the same face to the planet. As the moon orbits Earth, different parts of its face are illuminated by the Sun, leading to the linear phases. Due to their tidal interaction, the Moon recedes from Earth at the rate of approximately 38 mm/a (1.5m/year) over million of years, these tiny moderations &the lengthening of Earth's day by about 23 ms/yr - add up to significant changes. During the Ediacenan period, for example (approximately 620 Ma) there were 400 $\pm$7 days in a year, with each day lasting 21.9$\pm$0.4 hour.

The moon may have dramatically affected the development of life by moderating the Planet's climate. Paleontological evidence & computer simulation show that Earth's axial tilt is stabilized by tidal intercalation with the Moon. Some theorists think that without this stabilization against the torques applied by the sun & planets to Earth's equatorial bulge, the rotational axis might be chaotically unstable, exhibiting large changes over million of years, as is the case of Mars, though this is disputation.

Viewed from Earth Moon's directly sunlit portion illuminated. In common usage the four major phases are, the news the first quarter, the full moon & the last quarter A lunar month is the time between successive recurrences of the same phase due to the eccentricity of the Moon's orbits this duration is not perfectly constant but averages about 29.5 days.

Asteroids & Artificial Satellites

Earth's co-orbital asteroids population consists of quasi satellites, objects with a horseshoe orbit & trojans. There are atleast five quasi satellites.

As of September 2021, there are 4550 operational human made satellites orbiting Earth. There are also inoperative satellites, including vanguard 1, the oldest satellite currently in orbit & over 16,000 pieces of tracked space debris. Earth's longest artificial satellite is the International Space Station.

Earth Science

Physical characterstics

Size & shape

Earth has a rounded shape, with an average diameter of 12,742 km, making it the fifth largest planet of the solar system.

Earth due to its rotation it has the shape of an ellipsoid, bulging at its equator, its diameter is 43 km longer there than at its poles. Earths shape furthermore has local topographic variations. Though the largest local variation like a Mariana Trench (10,925 m below local sea level), only shortens Earth's average radius by 0.17 % & Mount Everest (8,484 m above sea level) lengthens it by only 0.14% parallel to the rigid land topography the ocean exhibits a more dynamic topography.

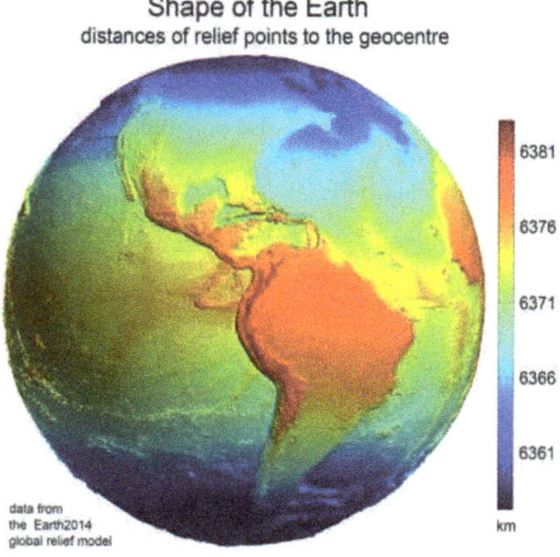

To measure the local variations of Earth's topography, geodesy employs an idealized earth producing a shape called geoid. Such a geoid shape is gained if the ocean is idealized. The result is smooth but gravitational irregular geoid surface providing mean sea level (MSL) as a reference level for topographic measure.

Surface

Earth's Surface is the boundary between the atmosphere & the solid Earth & Oceans. Defined in this way, Earths shape is an idealized spheroid - a squashed sphere - with a surface area of about 510 million km^2. Earth can be divided into two hemisphere, by latitude into the polar Northern & Southern hemispheres or by longitude Eastern & Western hemispheres.

Most of the Earth's surface is ocean water 70.8% on 361 million km^2. This vast pool of salty water is after called the world ocean. The world ocean is commonly divided into the Pacific ocean, Atlantic ocean, Indian ocean, Antarctic or Southern ocean, & Arctic ocean, from largest to smallest. The ocean covers the Earth's ocean crust, but to lesser extent with shelf seas also shelves of continental crust. The oceans crust form large ocean basins with features like abyssal plains, seamounts, submarine volcanoes, oceanic trenches, submarine canyons, oceanic plateaus & a globe spanning mid ocean - ridge system.

At Earth's polar regions, the ocean surface is covered by seasonally variable amounts of sea ice that often connects with polar land, permafrost & ice sheets, forming polar ice caps.

Earths land cover 29.2% or 149 million km^2 land of Earth's surface. The land surface includes many islands around globe, but most of the land surface is taken by the four continental landmasses, which are (in descending order): Africa, Eurasia, America (land mass), Antarctica & Australia (land mass). These land masses are further broken down & grouped into the continents. The Terrain of the land surface vows greatly & consists of mountains, desserts, plains, plateaus & other landforms. The elevation of the land surface varies from a low point of - 418 m at the Dead Sea, to a maximum altitude of 8,848 m at the top of Mount Everest. The mean height of land above sea level is about 797 m (2615 ft). Land can be covered by surface water, snow, ice, artificial structures or vegetation. Most of Earth's lands hosts vegetation, but ice sheets (10% not including the equally large land under permafrost) on cold as well as hot deserts (33%) occupy also considerable amounts of it.

The pedosphere is the outermost layer of Earth's land surface & is composed of soil & subject to soil formation processes. Soil is crucial for land to be arable. Earth's total arable land is 10.7 % of the land surface, with 1.3 % being permanent cropland Earth has an estimated 16.7 million km^2 of cropland & 33.5 million km^2 of pasture land.

The land surface & ocean floor form the top of Earth's crust, which together with parts of the upper mantle form Earth's lithosphere. Earth's crust may be divided into oceans & continental crust. Beneath the ocean floor sediments, the oceans crust is predominantly basaltic, while the continental crust may include lower density materials such as granite, sediments & metamorphic rocks. Nearly 75% of the continental surfaces are covered by sedimentary rocks, although they form about 5 % of the mass of the crust.

Earth's surface is continually being shaped by internal tectonic processes including earth quakes & volcanism; by weathering & erosion driven by ice, water, wind & temperature & by biological processes including the growth & decomposition of biomass into Soil.

Tectonic Plates

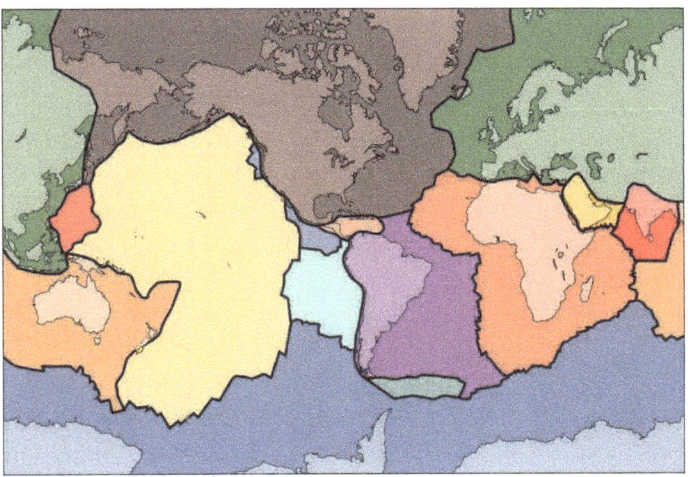

Earth's mechanically rigid outer layer of Earth's crust & upper mantle, the lithosphere, is divided into tectonic plates. These plates are rigid segments that move relative to each other at one of three boundaries types; at divergent boundaries two plates are pulled apart; at convergent boundaries, two plates come together; and at transform boundaries, two plates slide past one another laterally. Along these plate boundaries, Earthquakes, volcanic activity, mountain building &oceanic trench formation can occur. The tectonic plates ride on top of the acestherosphere, the solid but less viscous part of the upper mantle that can flow & move along with the plates.

As the tectonic plates migrate, oceanic crust is sub ducted under the leading edges of the plates at convergent boundaries. At the same time, the upwelling of mantle material at divergent boundaries create mid ocean ridges.

The seven major plates are the Pacific, North American, Eurasian, African, Antarctica, Indo - Australian and South American. Other notable plates include the Arabian plate, the Caribbean plate, the Nazca plate off the west coasts of south America & the scotia plate in the Southern Atlantic ocean. The fastest moving plates are the oceanic plate, with the cocos plates advancing at a rate of 75 mm/a (3.0 m/year) & the Pacific plate moving 52-69 mm/a (2.0 - 2.7 in/year). At the other extreme, the slowest moving plate is the South American plate, progressing at a typical note of 10.6 mm/a (0.42 in/year).

Internal Structure

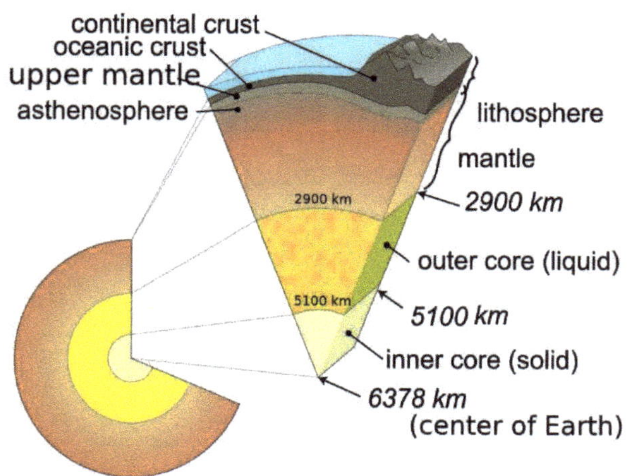

The Earth with radius of 6378/km is divided as from surface to center as Lithosphere (0-60 km) with less density, crust (0-35 km) with density 2.2-2.9, Upper mantle (35-660 km) with density 3.4-4.4, Lower mantle (660-2890 km) with density 3.4-5.6, Asthenosphere (100-700 km), Outer core (2890-5100 km) with density of 9.9-12.2, Inner core (5100-6378 km) with density of 12.8-13.1.

Earth's interior, like that of the other terrestrial planet, is divided into layers by their chemical or physical properties. The outer layer is a chemically distinct silicate solid crust, which is underlain by a highly viscous solid mantle. The crust is separated from the mantle by the Mohorovcic discontinuity. The thickness of the crust varies from about 6 km under the oceans to 30-35 km for the continents. The crust & the cold, rigid, top of the upper mantle are collectively known as lithosphere, which is divided into independently moving tectonic plates.

Beneath the Lithosphere is a Asthenosphere a relatively low viscosity layer on which the lithosphere rides. Important changes in crystal structure which the mantle occur at 410 km & 660 km below the surface, spanning a transition zone that separates the upper & lower mantle. Beneath the mantle, an extremely low viscosity liquid outer core lies above a solid inner core. Earth's inner core may be rotating at a slightly higher angular velocity than the remainder of the planet, advancing by $1 - 0.5^0$ per year, although both somewhat higher & much lower rates have also been proposed. The radius of the inner core is about one - fifth of that of Earth. Density increases with depth.

Among the solar planetary - sized objects Earth is the object with highest density.

Chemical Composition

Earth's mass is approximately 5.97×10^{24} kg. it is composed of iron (32.1% by mass), oxygen (30.1%) silicon (15.1%), magnesium (13.9%), sulfur (2.9%), nickel (1.8%), calcium (1.5%) & aluminum (1.4 %) with the remaining 1.2 % consisting of other elements. Due to gravitational separation, the core is primarily composed of the denser elements. Iron (88.8%) with smaller amounts of nickel (5.8%) sulfur (4.5%) & less than 1 % trace elements. The most common rock constituents of the crust are oxide over 99 % of the crust is composed of various oxides of eleven elements, principally oxides containing silicon (the silicate minerals), aluminum, iron, calcium, magnesium, potassium or sodium.

Internal Heat

The major heat producing isotopes within Earth are potassium -40, uranium -238 & thorium -232. At the center, the temperature may be up to 6000^0 C $(10,830^0$ F), & the pressure could reach 360 G pa (52 million psi).

The mean heat loss from Earth is 87 MW m^{-2}, for a global heat loss of 4.42×10^{13} W. A portion of the core's thermal energy is tempered toward the crust by mantle plumes, a form of convection consisting of upwelling's of higher - temperature rock. These plumes can produce hotspots & flood basalts. Move of the heat in Earth is lost through plate tectonics, by mantle up welling assosiated with mid - ocean ridges. The final major mode of heat loss is through conduction through the lithosphere, the majority of which occurs under the oceans because the crust there is much thinner than that of the continents.

Gravitational Field

The gravity of the Earth is the acceleration that is imparted to objects due to the distribution of mass within Earth. Near Earth's surface, gravitational acceleration is approximately 9.8 m/s^2. Local differences in topography, geology & deeper tectonic structure cause local & broad regional differences in Earth's gravitation field, known as gravity anomalies.

Magnetic Field

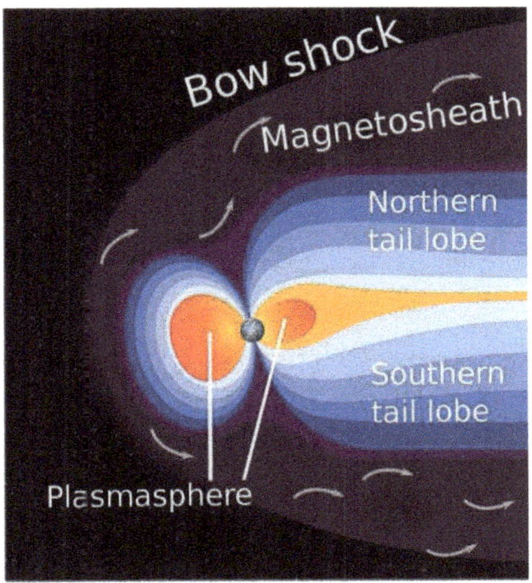

The main part of Earth's magnetic field is generated in the core, the site of a dynamo process that converts the kinetic energy of thermally & compositionally driven convection into electrical & magnetic field energy. The field extends outwards from the core, through the mantle & up to Earth's surface, where it is, approximately, a dipole. The poles of the dipole are located close to earth's geographic pole. At the equator of the magnetic field, the magnetic field strength at the surface is $3.05 \times 10^5 T$, with a magnetic dipole moment of $7.79 \times 10^{22} Am$, at epoch 2000, decreasing nearly 6% per century. The convection moments in the core are chaotic, the magnetic poles drift & periodically change alignment. This causes secular variation of the main field & field reversals at irregular intervals averaging a few times every million years. The most recent reversal occurred approximately 7,00,000 year ago.

The extent of Earth's magnetic field in Space define the Magnetosphere. Ions & electrons of the solar wind are deflated by the magnetosphere. Charged particles are contained within the magnetosphere; the plasmosphere is defined by low energy particles that eventually follow magnetic field lines as Earth rotates. The ring current is defined by medium energy particles that drift relative to the geomagnetic field, but with paths that are still dominated by the magnetic field, & the Van Allen radiation belts are formed by high - energy particles whose motion is essentially random but contained in the magnetosphere.

During magnetic storms & sub storms, charged particles can be deflected from the outer magnetosphere & especially the magneto tail, directed along field lines into Earth's ionosphere, where atmosphere atoms can be excited & ionized, causing the aurora.

Hydrosphere

Earth's Hydrosphere is the sum of Earth's water & its distribution. Most of the Earth's hydrosphere consists of Earth's global ocean. Earth's hydrosphere also consists of water in the atmosphere & on land, including clouds, island seas, lakes, rivers & underground water down to a depth of 2000 m.

The mass of the oceans is approximately 1.35×10^{18} metric tons. The oceans cover an area of 361.8 million km with a mean depth of 3682 m, resulting in an estimated volume of 1.332 billion km^3. About 97.5% of the water is saline; the remaining 2.5% is fresh water. Most fresh water about 68.7% is present as ice in ice caps & glaciers.

The remaining 30 % is ground water, 1% surface water (covering only 2.8% of Earth's land)& other small forms of fresh water deposits such as permafrost, water vapor in the atmosphere, biological binding, etc.

In Earth's coldest region, snow survives over the summer & changes into ice. The accumulated snow & ice eventually forms into glacier, bodies of ice that flow under the influence of their own gravity. Alpine glaciers form in mountainous areas, whereas vast ice sheets form over land in polar region. The flow of glaciers erodes the surface changing it dramatically, with the formation of U - shaped valleys & other land forms.

The average salinity of Earth's oceans is about 35 grams of salt per kilogram of seawater (3.5% salt). Most of this salt was released from volcanic activity as extracted from cool igneous rocks. The ocean are also a reservoir of dissolved atmosphere gases, which are essential for the survival of many aquatic life form. Sea water has an important influence on the world's climate, with the oceans acting as a large heat reservoir. Shifts in the oceanic temperature distribution can causes significant weather shifts.

The abundance of water, particularly liquid water, on Earth's surface is a unique feature that distinguishes it from other planets in the solar system. Solar system planets with considerable atmospheres do partly host atmospheric water vapor, but they lack surface conditions for stable surface water. Despite some Moons showing sign of large reservoirs of extraterrastrial liquid water, with possibly even more volume than Earth's ocean, all of them are large bodies of water under a kilometers thick frozen surface layer.

Atmosphere

The Atmospheric pressure at Earth's sea level averages 101.325 kPa, with a scale height of about 8.5 km. A dry Atmosphere is composed of 78.084 % nitrogen, 20.946 % oxygen, 0.934 % argon, & trace amounts of corban dioxide & other gaseous molecules. Water vapor content verses between 0.01% & 4% but averages about 1 %. Clouds cover around two thirds of Earth's surface more so over the oceans than land. The height of troposphere varies with latitude, ranging between 8 km at the poles to 17 km at the equators & seasonal factors.

Earth's biosphere has significantly altered its atmosphere. Oxygen photosynthesis evolved 2.7 gya, forming the primarily nitrogen - oxygen atmosphere today. This change enabled the proliferation of aerobic organisms & indirectly the formation of the ozone layer due to the subsequent conversion of atmosphere O_2 & O_3.

The ozone layer blocks ultraviolet solar radiation permitting life on land. Other atmosphere function important to life include transporting water vapor providing useful gases, causing small meter to burn up before they strike the surface, & moderating temperature. This last phenomenon is the green house effect trace molecules with the atmosphere serve to capture thermal energy emitted from the surface, thereby raising the average temperature. Water vapor, carbon dioxide, methane, nitrous oxide & ozone are the primarily green house gases in the atmosphere. Without this heat retention effect, the average surface temperature would be -$18°C(^0F)$ & life on Earth probably would not exist in its current form.

Weather & Climate

Earth's atmosphere has no definite boundary, gradually becoming thinner & fading into outer space. Three quarters of the atmospheres mass in contained within the first 11 km of the surface; this lowest layer is called the Troposphere. Energy from the Sun heats this layer, & the surface below, causing expansion of the air. This lower density air then rises & is replaced by cooler, higher density air. The result is atmospheric circulation that drives the weather & climate through redistribution of thermal energy.

Earth recieves $1361 w/m^2$ of solar irradiance. The amount of solar energy that reaches Earth's surface decreases with increasing latitude. At higher latitudes, the sunlight reaches the surface at lower angles & it must pass through thicker columns of the atmosphere. As a result the mean annual air temperature at sea level decreases by about 0.4^0C per degree of latitude from the equator. Earth's surface can be subdivided into specific latitudinal belts of approximately homogeneous climate. Ranging from the equator to the polar regions, these are the tropical, subtropical, temperature & polar climates.

Water vapor generated through surface evaporation is transported by circulatory pattern in the atmosphere. When atmospheric condition permits an uplift of warm, humid air, this water condenses & falls to the surface as precipitation. Most of the water is then transported to lower elevations by river systems & usually returned to the oceans or deposited into lakes. This water cycle is a vital mechanism for supporting life on land & is a primary factor in the erosion of surface features over geological periods. Precipitation pattern vary widely, ranging from several meters of water per year to less than a millimeter. Atmospheric circulation, topographic features & temperature differences determine the avg precipitation that falls in each region.

Upper Atmosphere

The upper atmosphere, the atmosphere above the troposphere, is usually divided into the Stratosphere, Mesosphere & Thermosphere. Each layer has a different lapse rate, defining the rate of change in temperature with height. Beyond these, the exosphere thins out into the magnetosphere, where the geomagnetic fields interact with the solar wind. Within the stratosphere is the ozone layer, a component that partially shields the surface from ultraviolet light & thus is important for life on Earth. The Kerman line, defined as 100 km above Earth's surface is a working definition for the boundary between the atmosphere & outer space.

Life on Earth

Earth is the only known place that has ever been habitable for life. Earth's life developed in Earth's early bodies of water some hundred million years after earth formed.

Earth's life has been shaping & inhabiting many particular ecosystem on Earth & has eventually expanded globally forming an overarching biosphere. Therefore, life has impacted Earth, significantly altering Earth's atmosphere & surface over long periods of time causing changing like the great oxidation Event.

Earth's life has over time greatly diversified allowing the biosphere to have different biomes which are inhabited by cooperatively similar plants & animals. The different biomes develops at distinct elevation or water depths, planetary temperature latitude & on land also with different humidity. Earth's species diversity & biomes reaches a peak in shallow waters & with forests particularly in equatorial, warm & humid condition while freezing polar regions & high altitudes, or extremely arid areas are relatively barren of plant & animal life.

Earth provides liquid water - an environment where complex organic molecules can assemble & interact, &

sufficient energy to sustain a metabolism. Plants & other organism take up nutrients from water, soils & the atmosphere. These nutrients are constantly recycled between different species.

Extreme weather, such as tropical cyclones (including hurricanes & typhoon), occurs over most of Earth's surface & has a large impact on life in those areas. On avg 11.800 death happens per years. Many places are subject to Earthquakes, land slides, tsunamis, volcanic eruption, tornadoes, blizzards, floods, droughts, wildfires & other calamities & disasters. Human impact is felt in many areas due to pollution of the air & water, acid rain, loss of vegetation, deforestation, desertification), loss of wildlife, species extinction, soil degradation, soil depletion & erosion. Human activates release green house gases into the atmosphere which causes global warming. This is driving changes such as the melting of glaciers & ice sheets, a global rise in average sea levels, increased risk of drought & wild fires, & migration of species to colder areas.

Past, Present, Future

Natural History

Formation

The oldest material found in the Solar system is dated 4.56 Ga (billion Years) ago. By 4.54 Ga the primordial Earth had formed. The bodies in the Solar system formed & evaded with the Sun. In theory, a solar nebula partition a volume out of a molecular cloud by gravitational collapse, which begins to spin & flatten into a circumstellon disk, & then the planets grow out of that disk with the Sun. A nebula contains gas, ice, gram & dust (including primordial nuclides). According to nebula theory, planetesimals formed by accretion, with the primordial Earth being estimated as likely taking anywhere from 70 to 100 million years to form.

Estimates of the age of the moon range from 4.5 Ga to significantly younger. A leading hypothesis is that it was formed by accretion from material loosed from Earth after a mars sized object with about 10 % of Earth's mass, named theia, collide with Earth.

After Formation

Earth's atmosphere & ocean were formed by volcanic activity & outgassing. Water vapor from these sources condensed into the oceans, augmented by water & ice from asteroids, protoplanets & comet. Sufficient water to fill the oceans may have been on Earth since it formed. In this model, atmospheric green house gases kept the ocean from freezing when the newly forming Sun had only 70 % of its current luminosity. By 3.5 Ga, Earth's magnetic field was established, which helped prevent the atmosphere from being stopped away by the solar wind.

New continental crust forms as a result of plate tectonics, a process ultimately driven by the continuous loss of heat from Earth's interior. Over the period of hundreds of millions of years, tectonic forces have caused areas of continental crust to group together to form supercontinents that have subsequently broken apart.

The most recent pattern of ice age began about 40 Ma & then intensified during the Aeistocere about 3 Ma. High & middle latitude region have since undergone repeated cycles of glaciation & thaw, repeating about every 21,000, 41,000 & 1,00,000 year. The last glacial period, colloquially called the "last ice age", covered large parts of the continents, to the middle latitudes in ice & ended about 11,700 year ago.

Origin of Life & Evolution

Chemical reactions led to the first self replicating molecules about four billion year ago. A half billion years later, the last common ancestor of all current life arose. The evolution of photosynthesis allowed the Sun's energy to be harvested directly by life forms. The resultant molecular oxygen (O_2) accumulates in the atmosphere & due to interaction with ultraviolet solar radiation, formed a protective ozone layer (O_3) in the upper atmosphere. True multicellular organs formed as cells within colonies became increasingly specialized. Aided by the absorption of harmful ultraviolet radiation by the ozone layer, life colonized Earth's surface. Among the earliest fossil evidence for life is microbial mat fossil found in 3.48 billion years old sandstone in western Australia.

During the Neoproterozoic, 1000 to 539 Ma, much of Earth might have been covered in ice. This hypothesis has been termed "Snowball Earth", & it is of particular interest because it preceded the Cambrian explosion, when multicellular life forms significantly increased in complexity. Following the Cambrian, 535 Ma, there have been at least five major mass extinction & many minor ones. Apart from the proposed current Holocene extinction ever, the most recent was 66 Ma, when on asteroid impact triggered the extinction of the non avian dinosaurs & other large reptiles, but largely spared small animals such as insects, mammals, lizards & birds. Manavalian life has diversified over part 66 mys& several million year ago on african ape species gained the ability to stand up right. This facilitated tool use & encouraged communication that provided the nutrition & stimulation needed for a larger brain which led to the evolution of humans. The development of agriculture & then civilization led to humans having an influence on Earth, & the nature & quantity of other life forms that continues to the day.

Future

Earth's expected long - term future is tied to that of the Sun. over the next 1.1 billion year, solar luminosity will increase by 10 % & over the next 3.5 billion year by 40 % increasing surface temperature will accelerate the inorganic Carbon cycle, reducing CO_2 concentration to levels lethally low for plants (10 ppm for C4 photosynthesis) in approximately 100-900 million years. The lack of vegetation will result in the loss of oxygen in the atmosphere, making animal life impossible. Due to the increased luminosity, Earths mean temperature may reach 100^0C (212^0F) in 1.5 billion year, & all ocean water will evaporate & be lost to space, which may trigger a runaway greenhouse effect, within the an estimated 1.6 to 3 billion year, even if the Sun were stable, a fraction of the water in the modern oceans, will descend to the mantle, due to reduced steam venting from mid - ocean ridges.

The Sun will evolve to become a red giant in about 5 billion years. Models predict that the Sun will expand to roughly 1 AU (150 million km), about 250 times its present radius. Earth's fate is less clear. As a red giant, the Sun will lose roughly 30 % of its mass, so, without tidal effects, Earth will move to an orbit 1.7 AU (250 million km) from the Sun when the star reaches its maximum radius otherwise, with tidal effects, it may enter the Sun's atmosphere & be vaporized.

Civilization

A Civilization is any complex society characterized by the development of the state, social stratification, urbanization & symbolic systems of communication beyond natural spoken language (namely a writing system).

Civilization are often characterized by additional features as well, including agriculture, architecture, infrastructure, technological advancement, a currency, taxation, regulation & specialization of labour.

Historically, a civilization has often been understood as a longer & "more advanced" cultures in implied contrast to smaller, supposedly less advanced cultures. In this broad sense, a civilization contrast with non - centralized tribal societies, including the cultures of nomad pastoralists neoliths societies, or hunter - gatherer however sometimes it also contrast with the cultures found within civilization themselves.

Civilizations are organized densely - populated settlements divided into hierarchical social classes with a ruling elite & subordinate urban & rural population, which engage in intensive agriculture, mining, small scale manufacturers & trade. Civilization concentrates power, extending human control over the rest of nature including over other human beings.

The word civilization relates to the Latin civitas or city. As the national geographic society has explained it; "this is why the more basic definition of the word civilization is a society made up of cities". The earliest emergence of civilization is generally connected with the final stages of Neolithic revolution in west Asia. Culminating in the relatively rapid process of urban revolution & state formation, a political development associated with the appearance of governing elite.

History

Examples for Civilization include, Mesopotamia, Khmer, Maya, Egyptians, Minoan, and the Inca. These Civilizations had, urban areas, surplus of food, a government and or religion, and a writing system. Natufran culture in the Levantine corridor provides the earliest case of a Neolithic revolution, with the planting of cereal crops attested from 11000 BCE The earliest Neolithic technology & lifestyle were established first in western Asia (for Example at Gobekis tepe, from about 9130 BCE), later in the Yellow river & Yangtze basins in china (for example the Peiligang & Pengtoushan cultures), & from these cores spread across Eurasia. Mesopotamia is the site of the earliest civilizations developing from 7400 years ago. This area has been evaluated by Beverly Milton Edwards as having "inspired some of the most important developments in human history including the invention of the wheel, the building of the earliest cities & the development of written course script". Similar pre civilized "Neolithic revolution" also began independently from 7000 BCE in north western south America (the coral Supe civilization) & in Mesoamerica. The black sea area served as a cradle of Europeans civilization. The site of Solnesata a prehistoric fortified (walled) stone settlement (prehistoric city) (5500 - 4200 BCE) - is believed by some archeology to be the oldest known town in present day Europe. Axial age the Bronze age collapse was followed by the Iron age around 1200 BCE, during which a number of new civilizations emerged, culminating in a period from the 8th to the 3rd century BCE which Karl Jaspers termed as the Axial age, presented as a critical transitional phase leading to classical civilization.

Modernity

A major technological & cultural transition to modernity began approximately 1500 CE in western Europe, & from this beginning new approaches to science & law spreadly around the world, incorporating earlier cultures into the technological & industrial society of the present.

Characteristics

Social scientists such a V Gordon Childe have named a number of traits that distinguish a civilization from other kinds of society. Civilization have been distinguished by these mean of subsistence, types of livelihood, settlement pattern, forms of government social stratification, economic systems, literacy & other cultural traits.

All civilization have depended on agriculture for subsistence, with the possible exception of some early civilization in Peru which may have depended upon maritime resource.

The traditional "surplus model" postulates that cereal forming results in accumulated storage & a surplus of food, particularly when people use intensive agriculture technique such as artificial fertilization, irrigation & crop rotation. It is possible but more different to accumulate horticultural productions & so civilization based on horticultural gardening have been very rare. Grain surpluses have been especially important because grain can be stored for long time.

A surplus of food permits some people to do thing besides producing food for a living, early civilization included soldiers, artisans, priests &priestesses, & other people with specialized careers. A surplus of food results in a division of labor & a defining trout of civilizations. However in some places hunter gatherer have had access to food surpluses, such as among some of the indigenous peoples of the pacific northwest & perhaps during the Mesolithic natufian culture. It is possible that food surpluses & relatively large scale social organization & division of labors predates plants & animal domestications.

Civilization have distinctly different settlement pattern from other societies the word civilization is sometimes defined as "living in cities". Non-formers, tend to gather in cities to work & to trend.

Compared with other societies, civilizations have a more complex political structure, namely the state. State societies: there is a greater difference among the social classes. The ruling class, normally concentrated in the cities, has control over much of the surplus & exercises its will through the action of a government or bureaucracy, Morton fried, a conflict theorist & human service, an integration theorist, have classified human cultured based on political systems & social inequality. This system of confiscation contains four categories.

- Hunter gatherer bonds, which are generally egalitarian.

- Horticultural - pastoralist societies in which there are generally two inherited social classes chief & commander.

- Highly stratified structure, or chiefdom, with several inherited social classes: king, noble, freeman, serf & slave.

- Civilization, with complex social hierarchies & organized institutional forms of government.

Economically, civilization display more complex patterns of ownership & exchange than less organized societies. Living in one place allows people to accumulate more personal persuasions than nomadic people some people also acquire landed property, as a private ownership of the land. Because a percentage of people in civilization do not grow their own food, they must trade their goods & services for food in market system, or receive food through the levy of tribute, redistributive taxation tariffs on other from the food producing segment of the population early human cultures functioned through a gift economy supplement by limited boater systems. By the early iron age, contemporary civilizations developed "money" as a medium of exchange for increasing complex transitions, In a village, the potter makes a pot for the brewer & the brewer cooperates the potter by giving him certain amount of beer. In a cities the potter may need new roof, the roofer may need new shoes, the blacksmith may need a new coat & the tanner may need a new pot these people may not be personally acquainted with one another & there needs may not occur all at the same time. A monetary system is a way of organizing these obligation to ensure that they are fulfilled. From the days of the earliest monetized civilization, monopoly controls of monetary systems have benefitted the social & political elites.

Writing, developed first by people in sumer is considered a hall mark of civilization & "appear to accompany the rise of complex administrative bureaucracies or the conquest state." Trader & bureaucrats relied on writing to keep accurate records. Like money, the writing was necessitated by the size of the population of a city & the complexity of its commerce among people who are not all personally acquainted with each other. However writing is not always necessary for civilization, as shown by the Inca civilization of the Andes , which did not use writing at all but except for a complex recording system consisting of knotted strings of different lengths & color: the "Quipus" & still functioned as a civilized society.

Aided by their division of labors & central government planning, civilization have developed many other diverse cultural traits. There include organized religion, development in the arts & countless new advances in science & technology.

Assessments of what level of civilization a polity has reached are based on the comparison of the relative importance of agricultural as opposed to trading or manufacturing capacities, the territorial extension of its power, the complexity of its division of labour & carrying capacity of its urban centres. Secondary elements include a developed transportation system, writing standardized measurement, currency, contractual & tort - based legal systems, art, architecture, mathematics, scientific understanding, metallurgy, political structures & organized religion.

Human Society

Origin of Humans dates back to 3,00,000 years ago near Africa, human have migrated to other part of the Earth since then & with advent of agriculture in the 10th millennium BC increasingly settling Earth's land. In the 20th century Antarctica had been the last continent is the only place with limited human presence.

Human population has since 19th century grown exponentially to seven billion in the early 2010, & is projected to peak on around ten billion in the second half of the 21st century.

Distribution & density of human population verses greatly around the world with the majority living in south to Eastern Asia & 90% inhabiting only the Northern hemisphere of Earth, partly due to the hemispherical predominance of the world's land mass, with 68% of the land mass being in the Northern hemisphere. Furthermore, since the 19th century humans have increasingly converged into urban areas with majority living in urban areas by the 21st century.

On the Earth surface Humans have lived by surface water resources near to rivers, lakes, underground water presence, depending more on fresh water resources, Beyond Earth's surface humans have lived on a temporary basis, with only special purpose deep underground & underwater presence, & a few space stations. Human population virtually completely remains on Earth's surface, fully depending on Earth & the environment it sustains since the second half of 20th century, some hundreds of human have temporarily stayed beyond earth, a tiny fraction of whom have reached another celestial body, the Moon.

Earth has been subject to extensive human settlement, & human have developed diverse societies & cultures. Most of Earth's land has been territorially claimed since the 19th century sovereign states (countries) separated by political borders & more than 200 such states (countries) exist today, with only parts of Antarctica & few small regions remaining unclaimed. Most of these states together form the United Nations, the leading worldwide intergovernmental organization, which

extends human governance over the ocean & Antarctica & therefore all of Earth.

Natural Resources & Land Use

Earth has resources that have been exploited by humans. Mainly renewable resources (Sunlight, Air, Water) & non renewable resources (Fossil fuels, coal, petroleum,natural gas) large deposits of fossil fuels are obtained from earth's crust, consisting of coal, petroleum & natural gas. These deposits are used by humans both for energy production & as feed stock for chemical production. Mineral ore bodies have also been formed within the crust through a process of ore genesis, resulting from action of magnetism, erosion & plate tectonics. These metals & other elements are extracted by mining, a process which often brings environmental & health damage.

Earth's biosphere produces many biological products for humans, including food, wood, pharmaceuticals, oxygen & the recycling of organic waste. The land - based ecosystem depends upon topsoil & fresh water. The oceanic ecosystem depends on dissolved nutrients washed down from the land. In 2019, 39 million km^2 of Earth's land surface consisted of forest

& woodlands, 12 million km^2 was shrub & garland, 40 million km^2 were used for animal feed production & grazing, & 12-14 % of ice - free land that is used for crop lands. 2 percentage points were irrigated in 2015. Human use building materials to construct shelter. Even the construction sector has grown exponentially by utilizing the minerals & producing construction materials.

Humans & the Environment

Human activities have impacted Earth's environments Through activities such as the burning of fossil fuels, humans have been increasing the amount of greenhouse gases in the atmosphere, altering Earth's energy budget & climate. It is estimated that global temperature in the year 2020 were 1-2^{0}C (2.2^{0}F) warmer than pre-industrial baseline. This increase in temperature, known as global warming have contributed to the melting of glaciers, rising sea levels, increased risk of drought & wildfire & migration of species to colder areas.

The concept of planetary boundaries was introduced to quantify humanity's impact on Earth. Of the nine identified boundaries, five have been crossed: Biosphere integrity, climate change, chemical pollution, destruction of wild habitats & the nitrogen cycle are thought to have passed the safe threshold. As of 2018, no country meets the basic needs of its population without transgressing planetary boundaries. It is thought possible to provide all basic physical needs globally within sustainable levels of resources use.

Lifestyle

The way of living life is termed as lifestyle. The culture, traditions are showcasing the lifestyle of societies passed on from generations to generation. Many cultures mainly worshipping the Earth as mother goddess & also worshiping the Sun, Moon etc. according to geological conditions. The traditions have been passed from generation to generation to adapt to seasonal changes of Earth, celebrate the life & to maintain a healthy lifestyle.

Every species of life beings living on Earth Animals, birds, other creatures pocess a lifestyle. Lifestyle mainly depends upon food & shelter. Human have the most evolved lifestyle than all other life beings. Humans have passed on their lifestyle in the form of tradition from generation to generation. Culture is the expression of lifestyle in many ways.

Culture

Culture in a concept that encompasses the social behavior, institution & norms, found in human societies, as well as the knowledge, beliefs, arts, laws, custom, capabilities & habits of the individuals in these groups. Culture is often originated from or attributed to a specific region or location.

Cultures is considered a central concept in anthropology, encompassing the range of phenomena that are transmitted through social learning in human societies. Cultural universals are found in all human societies. These include expressive forms like art, music, dance, ritual, religion & technologies like tool usage cooking, shelter & clothing. The concept of material culture cover the physical expressions of culture such as technology, architecture & art, whereas the immaterial aspects of culture such as principles of social organization (including practices of political organization & social institutions), mythology, philosophy, literature (both written & oral) & science comprise the intangible cultural heritage of a society.

When used as count noun a "culture" is the set of customs, traditions & values of a society or community. Such as an ethnic group or nation culture is the set of knowledge acquired over time. In this sense, multi culturals values the peaceful coexistence & mutual respect between different cultures inhabiting the same planet. Sometimes "culture" is also used to describe specific practices within a subgroup of a society, a subculture or counter culture. Within cultural anthropology, the ideology & analytical stance of cultural relativism hold that cultures cannot easily be objectively ranked or evaluated because any evaluation is necessarily situated within the value system of a given culture.

Cultural & Historical Viewpoint

Human cultures have developed many views of the planet. The standard astronomical symbol of Earth are a quartered circle, representing the four corners of the world, & a Globus cruiciger & Earth is sometimes personified as a deity. In many cultures the earth is a mother goddess that is also the primary fertility deity. Creation myths in many religions involve the creation of Earth by a supernatural deity or deities. The Gaia hypothesis developed in the mid - 20th century, compared Earth's environments & life as a single self regulating organism leading to broad stabilization of the conditions of habitability.

Images of Earth taken from space, particularly during the Apollo program, have been credited with altering the way that people viewed the planet that they lived on, called the overview effect, emphasizing its beauty, uniqueness & apparent frigility. In particular this caused a realization of the scope of effects from human activity on Earth's environment enabled by science, particularly Earth observation humans have started to take action on environment issues globally, acknowledging the impact of humans & the interconnectedness of Earth's environments.

Scientific investigation has resulted in several culturally transformation shifts in peoples view of the planet. Initial belief in a flat Earth was gradually displaced in ancient Greece by the idea of a spherical Earth, which was attributed to both philosophers pythogoras & pamenides. Earth was generally believed to be the center of the universe until 16th century, when scientists first concluded that it was moving object, one of the planets of the solar system.

It was only during the 19th century that geologists realized Earth's age was at least many million of years. Lord Kelvin used thermodynamics to estimate the age of Earth to be between 20 million & 400 million years in 1864, sparking a vigorous debate on the subject, it was only when radioactivity & radioactive dating were discovered in the late 19th& early 20th centuries that a reliable mechanism for determining Earth's age was established, proving the planet to be billions of billions of years old.